oxygen.
{stories}

ullie kowcun

oxygen.

DEDICATION

to you. in need of oxygen. my family. my friends.
complete strangers. thank you for your vulnerability.
thank you for cracking open a part of yourselves to
share with the world.
here are your lives. your blisses. your sorrows. thank
you for entrusting me with your stories.

TO:
_____

FROM:
_____

Copyright © 2018 Ullie Kowcun

All rights reserved.

ISBN-13: 978-1723308444

oxygen.

WARS.
for: luan

there were wars you never even knew
existed.
history books written beneath my chest.
i left because home wreaked of his breath;
his double fisted hands
that saved not an ounce of a place for me.
how every room reminded me
that she once lived there too.
and so i became a fighter,
a protector;
vigilant for the sake of peace.
and i returned-
but my limbs and mind were
dangling.
hello world war three
and liquor stained lips.
hello sleep without a roof
and girl without a name.
i could write hope in the sand
a thousand times
and a thousand times,
it washed away.
but here i am,
as imperfect as they come.
still growing.
setting my roots down.
and waiting for the blooms
those fragrant, summer blooms
that tell me i have yet to be enslaved
by any of this.

ullie kowcun

of all the wars i've ever fought,
the ones that waged
inside of me-
they lingered on the most.

oxygen.

SONGBIRD.
for: n.r.

there you were, a songbird, sitting in a coffee shop,
hair bundled up in streaks of light
that shone through the window
from the heavenly places.
i guess i knew too well that my soul
had found something.
something that felt familiar.
blessed.
like home.
my eyes cannot tell a lie
and so i found myself plunged deep
into the pools in front of me.
and for the first time,
i did not want to swim.
if this was drowning, then i did not want your ships
to save me.
perhaps i lingered too long.
perhaps i just did not want this to end;
how you painted my skin,
how we strummed our fingers through the pages
of a bookstore.
i still wonder at what could have been.
because i don't know where i lost you.
but i want you to know
that somewhere in between
the rows of these church pews,
sits a man, a little awkward and broken,
who would reach up and clutch the stars
just to see you again.

ullie kowcun

and i just wanted you to perch,
once more, where i could feel
your heartbeat.

oxygen.

GAPS.
for: manua

her heart fit perfectly into
the palm of my hand.
and i could have
left it there,
forever and a day,
beating life into my veins,
making me want to swim in
the rapids of her smile.
because every goodbye needed
a band-aid and
every morning i asked the sun
just to show me her face
with its rising.
even in the seconds
and hours of time
that daylight stole her from me,
i missed her.
my eyes blinked in a
different rhythm.
my fingers found air
in the gaps
where she belonged-
here, with me.
smiling.
dreaming.
being.

ullie kowcun

i missed her, even in the seconds
that it took for my lashes to
open and close;
for the light from the sun to
touch the wells of my eyes.

oxygen.

ABRACADABRA.
for: holly champion

i named him mercedes.
he was as black as the (k)night
that scrapes sky long after the sun has been left
to bleed out.
he spoke; muffler dragging, engine on but
disengaged.
always shrouded in a novel, well versed
with intermittent coughs, long days and history
books of untruths.
and i know now that those quiet, baby blues
would have robbed a bank for love.
but my heart became a cavern for things i have yet to
understand. and i wondered how i could miss a man
when there was
only a whisper of him left.
instead, magic glimmered around the brim of his hat
with slight of hand and one too many abracadabra's.
and all i ever wanted, was for him to remove the act,
take off the cape for once and sit awhile;
round bellied and laughing like a cloud
that had finally let go of rain.
undivided.
unforced.
clear-minded.
open to the exchange of souls.
open to listening to the pronouns and adjectives
in my sentences.
open to loving, half-broken.
but tomorrow was always the same
as yesterday.
so i asked him simply to remove his watch;
the gold infused keeper of silence,
the only fraction of time i would ever see-
and "leave it with me".

ullie kowcun

i only wanted to be all the magic
you ever needed.
the white rabbit you pulled from
your hat.
the opening and closing act.
and all the dazzling lights in
between.

oxygen.

GRAVITY.
for: anonymous

and sometimes i wondered
how we held so much depth,
how we plucked the universe
from gravity yet somehow still
understood that all we really needed
were forehead kisses,
soft rains
and a hammock to lay ourselves in.

ullie kowcun

we could not have one without
the other. the simple and
complex merely
wove themselves together.

oxygen.

MONSTERS.
for shelly

it hurts.
not because i did so much
but because every time you left
through the front door,
i wondered if i did enough.
don't get me wrong,
i'm about as far from a saviour
as an august moon in the
dead of winter.
but my love comes as fierce as my rage.
double dosed ferocity.
an ocean at storm.
for every beautiful mind
that walked its way into my life,
i felt one more wild-winged heartbeat.
and i knew if i could,
i would gather you in
to sleep safely underneath the very
folds of my skin.
to calm the hunt in your eyes
for just a little while longer.
it was never perfect.
and it was never easy.
the monsters
that settled in you,
became the beasts i had to slay.
and perhaps sometimes
you mistook me for them.
but it didn't matter if they
lived under the bed,
in the attic of your head

ullie kowcun

or in every single breath you took,
that made you go back
to that place.
because i loved you.
and maybe love had the power
to overcome all of this.
if it didn't,
i desperately wanted it to.
to replace your scars
with stars,
for even a brief passage of time.
it was you.
it was me.
it was us
against this world-
but together.
and i would do it
again.

oxygen.

UKELELE STRINGS.
for amy g.

this is for you
my flower child
my wild wind weaver
my little dancer
who never was but wanted to be
the one who grew to love and laugh
in basketfuls of berries
in plaid and fire and wine
and ukelele strings
you were always unusual in the most
enchanting ways
your hair tied up in some mysterious knot
and your eyes swirling with whimsical notion
it's funny because whether you were
brightly in love
or in your murkiest days
you had this reservoir of light
and when you needed it the most
it was already waiting -
already shining

ullie kowcun

you were windchimes.
you were stained glass windows.
you were light that could not
be dimmed.
everything about you was eternal-
even on the days you felt like
a distant star; burning somewhere,
in a far-off galaxy.

oxygen.

HOME.
for: j.r.

you were my house.
and for awhile i really believed
that the only walls around us
were made of the gardens;
in the front yard-
in the backyard-
and in the deep wells of my chest.
somehow you managed to
take my hummingbird heart
and cease it from rupturing
altogether.
the caution tape i had tangled
severely around my body,
loosened its grip
and i found myself believing
that maybe i was someone
worth holding onto.
maybe i could trust again.
maybe i was kind after all.
i fell into you like a blanket;
soft and present and i
wrapped myself in everything
i thought we were.
i still don't know why you
injured me so.
why as soon as i hung up
the drapes and filled the pantry
with possibilities,
you said, "game over"
and folded in.

ullie kowcun

and if the earth had felt
my ribs that day,
winter surely would have fallen.
so i became a chair,
rocking to soothe my own
disbelief.
and i was reduced to this;
purging my gut from
any remains that attempted
to linger.
embracing bathroom stalls
and feverishly washing
the vomit from the insides
of my jeans just to feel
the acid burn and remind myself
that i was still awake.
still breathing.
and i thought i would never
be the same. and the truth is,
i wasn't.
i could no longer find
the human that i once was.
but one day i saw her,
like a friend i had always
wanted to meet.
and she was dancing.
she was singing.
she was making art of her words.
and i knew that the only home
i ever needed,
was inside of myself.

oxygen.

CAKE.
for: a.h.

we were two butterflies,
you and i.
finding ourselves.
finding freedom.
and finding first love.
but you were a monarch and
i was a glasswing.
and for a year we tried;
against every tide and
every hand of cards we
were dealt,
against the bitter winds
and brazen sun,
we tried.
and when you left home
to come to me
to come to us, i couldn't have
wanted anything more.
and if love had a name
it would have sounded just like
our wings whisking away
at dusk.
starting new.
breathing in synchronized
breaths.
but on my sixteenth birthday,
among cake and laughter,
the most of my heart
shattered to pieces.
one phone call;
with your father in your ear,
and everything changed.

ullie kowcun

how abruptly my flight
was halted.
twenty-three years i wandered
aimlessly.
pretending at love.
drinking at life as though i
could wish it away,
bury my grief.
i could not.
with my head on my pillow
and in dreams that only light
can explain, i saw it.
it was not meant for now.
it was not meant for this earth.
perhaps our love was too great
for the human world.
perhaps in another time-
another place.

oxygen.

RED.
for: shannon bucht

i am a lover.
a heart that poured itself out
like room temperature red,
bleeding at the seams
to let you drink.
and i was happy.
i really was.
first loves and wine
always seemed like
the perfect pairing
and so i lost myself in a dream
that i could not wake up from.
and most of the time,
i did not want to.
but some days i sipped
of wanting more-
not more from you,
but more of me.
so young we were
so deep.
and we knew nothing else
but us.
i let go because i needed to.
because sometimes freedom
comes in the unknown places.
sometimes life begins
when another ends.
and sometimes the loss
is worth it all.

ullie kowcun

alone is not always abandoned.
sometimes it is a sprout,
inching its way through.
being brave against the soil-
finding sun.

oxygen.

OH CHILD.
for: anonymous

i never gave you a name.
but i carried you like vintage glass.
my body, the hands that held
every detail of your delicate making.
legs that ran through fields
and climbed up mountains.
hands that played on merry-go-rounds
and built castles of sand to reach to the sky.
i imagined your smile was as wide
as the ocean was deep.
i knew you would be a giver.
a lover.
a lender of light.
but fifteen weeks did not let me
show you to the sun.
fifteen weeks did not let my hips
grow to honour your arrival.
fifteen weeks took your grave
and made it a home in my very own bones,
where i cried until i did not
think there were tears left to fall.
oh child. i loved you already then,
as though you were sitting on my lap
on a sunday afternoon,
finding shapes in the clouds
and asking to stay up a little
while longer.

ullie kowcun

so here i'll sing my lullabies
my softest voice, my simmered sighs.
you'll wait for me in heaven's skies.
our separate ways were not goodbyes.

oxygen.

FIRES.
for: dennis

how is it that one day
we are toasting the bride
and the very next
we see the clinging to life,
the shallow streams of breath
that halt their trickle.
how is it that the same flesh
can hold both love
and utter mourning;
bones that laugh
like an accordion
and weep like a siren
on tiffany street.
how do i dream in colour
when i keep
fading into shades.
these fires.
some warm my hands
and others
break my heart.

ullie kowcun

sometimes the sun shines
and sometimes it rains.
sometimes i wonder
if it's all the same.
i might dance on the water
or sink in a bleeding sky but
as long as i'm breathing,
i guess i'm alive.

oxygen.

FLIGHT.
for: jim

once in awhile words cling to
the tip of my tongue
because everything i want to say
becomes deficient
like iron in the blood
weakening me to the knees
this indescribable marriage
of wild frenzy and calm
a thousand miles of skies
that sing to me in harmony
with the baritone of the engine
sunsets arranged meticulously
as though they are laid out for me
and i in my child-like wide eyed wonder
become entangled in the art
of the heavens i am in
and the sundry of tiny towers
speckled at my feet
like standing in a lonely field
and looking up at the galaxies
yet not feeling lonely at all
because i am a part of it
the great vastness that pulls me in
from this magnificently winged creature
and for the first time in my life
in the solitude of space and time
i am home.

ullie kowcun

i carried wings upon my back
and there they grew,
so on the days i could not walk,
i simply flew.

oxygen.

THICKETS.
for: winona

of all these constellations
wide open fields of endless wheat
complex cities and skyscrapers
intersecting highways
weaving in and out
in and out
sun splayed days
and lampposts on the edge of streets
you did not meet me there
not where the light shone bravely
but in the deepest tree-laced thickets
and i
a corpse who'd lost her words and way
who could no longer speak
soul in a heap
you rescued me
while there in your own quiet misery
and ocean depths of tragedy
past all your dreadful childhood ghosts
an angel
made of earth to show me
that kindness is not confined
to an easy life
and love shows up here
even at the brink of losing
everything

ullie kowcun

she was a beacon,
carving light into my shoulders.
a fresh bouquet,
still rooted in the earth of her
own sunlessness.

oxygen.

STAIRWELLS AND LIGHT.
for: charity

hey beautiful girl
one house down
in the same town
why didn't i
hear you crying
then
there must have been
some light coming in through
the cracks
because they don't walk like you do
when it's all painted black
hey beautiful girl
look at me
from your balcony
yeah no blue
is gonna hold you
down
you must have had
your will and your suitcase
packed
a thousand times in the stairwell
where it's all painted black
but this is love
when the river flows
instead of folding in
and this is love
when the stars still rise
in a broken heaven
and when you're running
out of air
and it settles you
back there
you'll give your breath away
think i already know

ullie kowcun

and when the heavy
words speak
on pages long and deep
you will lay them down softly
think i already know
hey beautiful girl
your eyes show
what your lips don't know
it looks like
you might make it
there must have been
some light coming in
through the cracks
because they don't walk like you do
when it's all painted black
but this is love
when the river flows
instead of folding in
and this is love
when the stars still rise
in a broken heaven
hey beautiful girl
one house down
in the same town

oxygen.

COMPOSED.
for: drw.

my heart does not break anymore.
it does not fracture, sink or fall.
there is no longer gleaning there
from summer's skies and blossom's call.
i cannot hear the ocean's rumble
nor see the faintest, glimmering light.
somewhere i lost the last of it;
the holding on with soldier's fight.
clutched in these fists in fragments now
to a captive audience portrayed
this self-composed, melodious man;
(the most extravagant charade).
i hold my head high, rise to bow.
if home still lives, it's there,
lost in the notes, the treble clefs
and the valiant fanfare.
but only in visible seconds and ounces,
only in seemingly sweet conversation,
only in counterfeit, crumbling concoctions
and moments of gin and tonic salvations.
to this very day, in deep, crowded spaces,
in soft bedside longings and seasides of faces,
i reach for her skin - the dream that i'm in.
the sunset.
the stars.
the moonlight.
the hill.
perhaps there,
she's loving me still.

ullie kowcun

and maybe one day
i would find air.
tangible enough to grasp.
sweet enough to put to my mouth.
but potent enough to save me.

oxygen.

SCARS.
for: alex

there were many hours that day.
they were strenuous.
they were sun baked and grueling.
flesh and brain,
prodded past limits.
aching for victory;
praying for salvation from this longevity;
this black belted extravaganza
of "how much can you endure?".
i could not avoid the hook
as it took me down to my knees
and sprawling across the floor.
body in a heap.
i lay.
motionless yet otherworldly.
and in this dark, i came upon a quest.
time traveling back to all the
wretchedness,
to my abuser, eye to eye.
to courage and forgiveness.
i wanted desperately to return
the scars and say, "here, i am,
take these, they are yours to
suffer with now".
but oh my wise, strong soul.
it flew me there to enunciate
the words in large, bold print-
"i feel pain, therefore i am,
i cannot run from its source
or hide to ignore it".
it moved me.
not to tears but to empowerment.
to waking up and rising to my rival,

ullie kowcun

ready.
fierce.
brave hands.
superman.

> pain was never my enemy.
> it was wishing it away,
> that had me misconstrued.

oxygen.

DEAR KILLER.
for: amy

you were a spear.
and my heart severed a thousand times
for every knock on the door that i replayed
in my head from that day forward.
the brave voice that tried to tell me
i was widow.
i was storm.
i was void that would not end.
like a clap of thunder-
gone.
like chaos without reason.
rainwater without a basin
to catch the falling.
dear killer.
i did not wake from my sleep on the couch
with his mouth, drizzling upon my cheek.
i did not hear his voice spill love into my bones
and i could not shake the thought that night
or any other night, of his last minutes
and the days and hours and years
you withdrew from him.
from us.
and there in the dark, i built my home on emptiness.
i hung death on every wall like a vivid piece of art
so that i could not walk past it without the heavy
reminder
that i was here
and he was absent.
that i was left to come to a screeching
halt at a stop sign that should
never have existed.
that my children were broken and
bent and fatherless.
dear killer.

ullie kowcun

i am not finished yet.
there were days that i wanted to die.
there were days i would have caught the bullets
with my bare, clenched teeth
and driven them back into your skull.
but there were days that i knew
i needed to love and dream and
forge a path to forgiveness.
dear killer.
even when the weather turns
and the smell of an open field
brings him back to me;
to the future we had planned,
to the vacant cavity of my chest,
you will not get a two for one deal.
dear killer.
i love harder now because of your inadequacies.
dear killer.
your meager attempts will not keep me from knowing
that blessings still travel in disguises.
dear killer.
you have not ended me.

> i am not resurrected, no.
> not from the parts that died.
> but i chose to breathe in
> all the good
> and exhale the darker side.

oxygen.

GLOW.
for: jen

some words are better left unsaid.
i was hurt.
vines grew unkempt and wild
and climbed up into my bedframe
every time i closed my eyes.
you see, trauma is a six letter word for,
"do not touch me"
and i made a cardboard sign to warn you
that i was fragile turned inside out.
i was emotion smothered with ink.
i was, "i wish i could feel but i am too afraid to".
so i found someone
who adored his own reflection
more than mine,
so that he could only love me from afar.
because maybe that is what i needed
and maybe that is all i deserved.
ten years in the shadows of a mirror
and four more in the darkness
with a heart accused of winter.
and if i was ever cold, it was only because
i could not find how to give
with tender breath.
to break myself open would be
to crack the very parts of me
that may seep through.
the ones i had to stitch into the insides
of my gut just to feel safe from the world-
the world.

ullie kowcun

it always made me feel different.
unusual.
misplaced somehow.
but my heart? it exists.
just as the moon with its
effervescent glow.
i am here.
i am growing with the tides.
i am choosing not to be afraid.
not anymore.

so then,
i will take all these things
and carve them into my soul.
the scars, the tears and the light
that clambers my skin to remain.

oxygen.

STRANGER.
for: lauren

there was something about him
and even now, i cannot put his soul
into words-
not justifiable ones.
he was christmas lights in july
and a summer day in the dead of winter.
all i knew was that he had somehow
managed to string a medley of
constellations into me.
i could not help but wonder if i would
see him again tomorrow and if he would
still shine in the same, bright way.
but he did.
he always did.
and i had never dreamed i would
see the day that i would pull out
my chemistry set and blush
at the mere thought of science again.
but i saw him weave his magic into
everyone else too.
wild ones and soft ones.
the old and broken and discarded ones.
the minimum wage but happy ones.
he was the stranger you wanted to meet.
the charm you wanted to pull in
just a little closer to your chest.
and perhaps he made my heart beat
out of rhythm for awhile.
but oh how beautiful,
the tired mouths, that were simply made
to smile.

ullie kowcun

he stopped at nothing
to make me smile.
and my mouth curved up like a tide
that never wanted to let go
of the shore.

oxygen.

SYLLABLES.
for: anastasia

i was misplaced.
fairy dust on my fingertips
and rose petal eyes.
a gypsy soul amongst
skyscrapers edging their way
into everything
i was not.
when i tried to belong,
i was crimson in a sea
of quintessential blue.
half stumbling into the universe
and half trailing off into
unknown places.
noticeably unnoticed.
heart hanging loosely
off my sleeve,
willing myself to take
the colours of my brain
and paint something for once.
my own version of art.
my own wings,
flying to music and syllables
unheard by most ears.
this divergence,
my sacred calling.
my sweet mother tongue.

ullie kowcun

i was made of earth
and autumn leaves.
old tire swings and rivers that
needed only to flow.

oxygen.

THIS.
for: rose

this
i cannot
all my limbs dangling
in cobblestone
so recklessly arched
into the ungreat beyond
surprisingly caught
handcrafted or dark scheme
devised
so hauntingly like slavery
is this the whip
after which we sought

this
i cannot
medley of bruises
on a platter
the clock synchronized
with the pounding in my flesh
tumultuous clot
dire veins circulating
the truth
deciphering validity
is this the draw
and i won the lot

ullie kowcun

this
i cannot
my suit of birthdays
turned inside out
uncensored and scathed
split open to the bare lines
and desperate to blot
hold onto the cold bed frame
find breath
my spirit and gethsemane
is this the sun
that the giver brought

oxygen.

SEAHORSE.
for: anonymous

only yesterday you were born
a seahorse in my stationary arms
and purely out of instinct
i became a pendulum
to swing you out of high waters
and far away from suffocating streets
and crumbling alleys
when your eyes became a river
i lifted every stone to shut the gate
you broke into my world
and stole both chambers
left and right
and i wasn't afraid
because everything i had ever lived for
culminated the minute i held you
words became lyrics
and songs became an orchestra
that made me feel like i was in
the presence of angels
every evening my heart fell with the sun
at saying goodnight
we counted the stars
i stroked your head and healed your wounds
every morning i woke with your sweet breath
at my shoulders sustaining me
as the tide flowed in over my feet
everything was less than i would offer
and nothing was more than i would give
cumbersome knew not my satchel
and laden dripped not from my lips
hands turned and cities rose and fell
i was perilously perfect and meticulously flawed
i swam and i sank
i tried

ullie kowcun

i really tried
i second guessed the pinnacle of my calling
how could i be deciphered as an anecdote
without a punchline
where were the arms that held you in their rhythm
that cradled this river horse from monsters and
ghosts
and climbed up every mast to become a shield
against the wind that stirred up and cursed in your
face
which funnel stole the music that kept you close to
the shore
my spine was wounded and my satchel tore beneath
the weight
i hastily gathered everything i knew
and threw it back into my chest
and purely out of instinct i became a pendulum
to swing you out of high waters
and far away from suffocating streets
and crumbling alleys
when your eyes became a river
i lifted every stone to shut the gate
you broke into my world and stole both chambers
left and right
and i wasn't afraid
because everything i had ever lived for
culminated the minute i held you
again

oxygen.

ICE.
for: francesca gray

you were still a child in my eyes,
too young for hands dusted with chalk
and a glass full of ice.
i wouldn't have wished this on anyone.
how your sweet eyes turned into empty rooms.
long and narrow hallways of weeping willows
with thirty minute intervals of erratic bliss.
it took you from me.
it took you from your babies.
and shaved twenty years from your dreams.
but there wasn't a night that i wouldn't have
cradled you back in my arms.
held you close.
told you i loved you like the day
i first laid your little body against my chest.
there wasn't a mountain i wouldn't have moved.
or an ocean i wouldn't have crossed.
because love doesn't end at crystals
dripping from your tongue.
love doesn't run from open sores
and simmering flesh.
but those mistakes have haunted me.
and i can't say that it was ever easy.
to make myself a mother to my grandchildren.
to watch you escape into someone i hardly knew.
this beautiful and perfect flower
wilting right in front of me.
and i ever only wanted to be the water
that brought you home.
that made you smile.
that grew you back into love with yourself.
my heart will not be bare of you.
it keeps you, still. even here and now.
after all of this.

ullie kowcun

i will keep on loving every petal
of you.
the ones that stay.
the ones that fall.
the ones that do not bloom at all.

oxygen.

BREATHE.

oh world
have we not yet begun
to understand
feet shuffling like cattle
to slaughter
the nine to five rise and shine
the sweet and sour of daily grind
the figuratively speaking
blind
we are bound more than ever
even in all that we have
freedom pounds its fist through
the windowpanes of our souls
we think we have mastered it
the secret to happiness
our brave smiles conjuring up
fiction-
breathe
inside we want only this
to be found
to be loved
to be carried around like tenderness
your aches are not weakness
they are not a lash for your sins
grip onto this
carve it into your skull
hear it like a flower's fragrant bloom
you
are
not
alone

ullie kowcun

do not speak
in melodious sonnets
to a world whose mother tongue
is tragedy.

oxygen.

OXYGEN.

if i could place you here
resuscitate some life back
in your sunken chest
if i could cause your limbs to move
with freedom
find your feathers
fly awhile
this your flask of oxygen
a tree drunk on sun
an open field flooded with grain
the endless skies
that do not hesitate to be your movie screen
those rich and fertile shades of blue
the ancient night with its celestial stars
drink this
the air is plentiful and deep
inhale the sweet of falling rain
caress the downpour on your skin
the soul of your dear hangover
your new awakening

ullie kowcun

and so i asked the trees
to waltz with me.
one final dance
before i made my bed in their
oxygen.
for i was alive now,
still broken, yes. but with dreams
on my taste buds again.

Printed in Great Britain
by Amazon